UNRAVELING SUNLIGHT

By Joe Barca

Joe Barca

Published in the United States of America by Joe Barca Books

Copyright © Joe Barca 2020

ISBN: 978-0-578-71582-7

No part of this book may be used or reproduced in any manner whatsoever without written permission except in the case of brief quotations embodied in critical articles or reviews.

This book is dedicated to Susan, Brendan, and Alex.

Previously Published Inclusions

The following poems – or versions of them – were originally published in the following publications listed.

Empty - The Literary Yard 2018
Invisible – Light Through the Mist 2018
Steady Me – Vita Brevis 2019
News Cycle – Pangolin Review 2019
Cherished – Pangolin Review 2019
Holiday – Pangolin Review 2019
Untitled – From Whispers to Roars 2019
Brooklyn – From Whispers to Roars 2019
Pools – Vita Brevis Poetry 2019
Depth – Selcouth Station Press 2018
Sensory – Selcouth Station Press 2018

Contents

Page 9	Introduction
Page 13	Loss
Page 14	Non-Linear
Page 15	Empty
Page 16	Don't Touch Me Today
Page 17	Addicted
Page 18	Heartbreak
Page 19	Blown
Page 20	Invisible
Page 21	Steady Me
Page 22	Startle
Page 23	Goodbye
Page 24	Skyless
Page 25	Intoxication
Page 26	Demons
Page 27	I look for you
Page 28	Untitled
Page 29	Nursery
Page 30	News Cycle
Page 31	I am sinless (I think)

Page 33	Gone
Page 34	World War III
Page 35	She's Gone
Page 36	Cherished
Page 37	Mistletoe
Page 38	Hungry
Page 39	Alone
Page 40	Shine
Page 41	Uplifting
Page 42	Behind the Scenes
Page 43	Holiday
Page 44	Untitled
Page 45	December
Page 46	Brooklyn
Page 48	Secret
Page 49	Untitled
Page 50	Hope Street
Page 51	Bubbling
Page 52	Shepherd
Page 53	Twilight
Page 54	Frozen
Page 55	Fanfare

Page 56	Turning
Page 57	Labyrinth
Page 58	Pools
Page 59	Maybe I Was Wrong
Page 60	Springtime in New England
Page 61	My Haven
Page 62	Liberation
Page 63	The Storm
Page 64	Starlit
Page 65	Virginia Woolf
Page 66	Bathing
Page 67	Violets
Page 68	Polaroid
Page 69	Depth
Page 70	Not Fancy
Page 71	Love Song
Page 72	A Meadow of Junes
Page 73	Sensory
Page 74	Untitled
Page 75	Winning
Page 76	Collide
Page 77	Company

Page 78	Awakening
Page 80	Desperation
Page 81	Aubade
Page 82	Folly
Page 83	Innocence
Page 84	Nature
Page 85	What is truth?
Page 86	Sinking
Page 88	Untitled
Page 89	Untitled
Page 90	Divination
Page 91	Solstice
Page 92	Untethered
Page 93	I love you
Page 94	Molecular
Page 95	Acknowledgements
Page 97	Poet Biography

Introduction

I started writing poetry about seven years ago, using Twitter as my experimental laboratory. Currently, I try to post "a poem a day" on social media.

Anyone wondering about my inspiration as a poet should know that I have become obsessed with the following collections: *Afterland* by Mai Der Vang, *Book of Hours* by Kevin Young, *Mouthful of Forevers* by Clementine von Radics, and *Twenty Love Poems* and a *Song of Despair* by Pablo Neruda. I am also addicted to many poems in the *Best of American Poetry* which is released annually.

The poetry in this collection flows from darkness into light. I hope that you enjoy the journey.

Joe Barca

UNRAVELING SUNLIGHT

By Joe Barca

Joe Barca

Loss

dear friend,
hold me tightly

because black holes
are deep and I don't hear
the music on the radio
anymore

Non-Linear

blood and water

mother, husband, holy daughter

we don't always grow

in vertical lines

and sometimes we die

in circular confusion

but the Canadian geese

fly south in chevrons

and the starlings rhyme

in swooping intricate patterns

- and we carry on

Empty

There's a certain heartbreak in clothes that lay folded too neatly
in the wardrobe; in a ghost that inhabits the closet.
He lives in a home that is wounded. The floorboards are
  quietly weeping.
He is half of a couple, holding a yard sale for a needy heart.
Now and then he sees his wife in the face of a stranger.
He hears her voice on the answering machine and it lingers.
And he has too many casseroles stacked in his freezer.

Don't Touch Me Today

I am paper

and you are glass

I am poetry

and you are fiction

Addicted

she was the opioid girl

with promised wings

she was trampled flowers

in fertile green

she was a stream of elegies

and primrose prose

her eyes were bright

shallow graves

she often dated ruins

of pretty boys

her dress was elegant

her heart, maculate

she would mainline

blue skies all day long

she was hope

choking

Heartbreak

and the moon
slides into the ocean

the sky is painted
inky black
she pulls away
from him

all things must end
- even devotion

Blown

I held you
like a fistful of dandelions

but the wind blew tragedy
in the face of permanence

in the face of my arrogance
and the lies I tell myself at night

we all return to ground.

Invisible

My home is a plastic bag. My food is the scraps
of your universe. You do not see me,
but my heart breathes. I have no hope,
but I have my integrity. There is a flame
in my mind. Can you help me?
Just until I can stand.
My past is not the future
Believe in me. Please.

Steady Me

I press my hands to the ribs

of your past. All things uneven.

Crows screech. And I hold the wire. Unsteady.

My mother told me that you marry

a family. But I only want a community of you.

All of this incompleteness

and all of these expectations.

We stock a shelf with the clay of our hearts.

Startle

A deer emerges in my headlights –
a thud. My spirit animal is bleeding –
out. Every death – a domino.
This boulder on my chest is wailing.

Snow drifts – I am madness.
My heart is a fawn orphaned.
If I could choke back the river,
I would swallow this story.

Goodbye

The raindrops are long
and the mirror is gray.

The trees have stripped
the cold white souls

from the low hanging sky.
Even the crows are quiet,

for they are the pallbearers
on this funereal day.

Skyless

when she goes quiet

I pray:

what can I do?

It's a punishing darkness.

I could turn away;

write her off, but she was

a forgiveness

a gift

a second chance.

        So I

                hang

                        on.

Intoxication

She presses her lips
close to the ear

of my imagination.
A universe breathes in.

A skinscape of confessions.
No prison for self-control.

I whisper a prayer to the god
of drunken bodies.

If only it was alcohol.
What do you take

when you're hungover
from falling under?

Demons

Let's have the voices in my head
hang out with the voices in yours.

Let the ghosts haunt the halls.
We'll sever the limbs of rumination.

You and I will inhabit a world
where every moment is still and emptiness, full

I Look for You

in winter's light,

when the earth is barely breathing.

In the soft gray bloom of clouds,

I grieve the cost of leaving.

Untitled

they said she was a classic beauty
but love is not made of porcelain

and nobody dared
hold her

Nursery

he chases secret magpies
down Hickory Lane

"One for sorrow
Two for joy"

"Three for a girl"
he sits on his mother's lap
a time traveler

at forty-three
he still recites it

"Four for a boy"

she is gone
but the verses remain

a parliament cries out
the glitter of her name

News Cycle

On her cell phone
the world is up in flames

outside, white rain falls.
Her children fly with snow angels

and their wheaten terrier
runs crop circles, spinning mindful.

I am sinless (I think)

Opaque screen.
Velvet light.

Dust dancing.
Bless me father.

I make things up.
I hit my sister.

I swore at my mother.
I ate meat on Friday.

Then I must confess.
that my confessions

are lies.

I kneel at the altar.
The marble is hard.

My elbows falter.
Five Our Fathers.

Ten Hail Marys.
An Act of Contrition.

I try to separate
my god from religion.

Gone

she walks by my house
without her golden retriever
– again

her body talks
I speak to God

how can I mourn the loss
of an animal that I don't even know

my pup runs out
to lick her face

a gentle rain falls

World War III

people act strangely
when Paris dies

all the lovers
become automatons

every wedding bell
a silent gong

the kiss becomes the coroner
and lips announce the wailing sounds

all the fingers cling
to tangled vines

it's not until
the river rises

that the emptiness
becomes a swan

She's Gone

all these winters pass
dogwoods shock
squirrels chase

it's nearly the spring
and seedlings pop
oh, little suitcases of hope

a rake, a hoe, and a trowel
dirt filled fingernails
- my mother

Cherished

ivory memories fall
from New England Skies

in December

a sled, a snowman,
and a shiver of stars.

Mistletoe

This year I'm going to string the lights from your ribcage.
Red and green, but mostly white.
Because the hope of reconciliation
twinkles, despite.

And I don't need a rush of gold.
I just want to touch the interstices
between the starlings and your night sky.

Hungry

December breaks

reluctance fades

two mouths meet

between

the silence

and the snow.

Alone

sometimes a breakup is a gift
a good death

but it's difficult to "unknow"
your name

so I take coffee to the lake
and taste the monastic

Shine

she looks away

and he slips sunlight

into her pocket

Uplifting

my favorite poem

is a kite string

that secures the moon

to your ribcage

Behind the Scenes

You cannot know a heart
on a stage spun from gold.

The curtain descends.
Lights begin to dim.

Not until makeup is removed
and the audience has gone home

will you see her face,
a clarity, a glow.

Holiday

all souls are windows / children paint the Christ child / a stray dog lifts her leg to yellow / Acela Express surges into town / a thousand buoys bob / an infant in a baby sling drops her mitten / a glass is raised /a local bar hums / the town drunk is born again in hair of tinsel / hung along the silver-coated pane

Untitled

She is drunk
on the beauty

of lonely mountains.
And on certain days

the chime of church bells.
The concrete bench

in the center of town.
A perch for angels.

She paints metaphorical daises
on the shadows

of passing strangers.

December

We stroll along hand in hand. Window shopping.
We watch white doves invade a snow globe.
How did they enter?

A cage, reversed.
A freedom of winters.
They skate on icy ribbons.

>A murmuration.
>
>A mystery.

God pirouettes with miracles.

Brooklyn

between the kisses
and the dance floor
sits a DJ

it's 2 AM
and we're drinking
uptown

all our
New Year's Resolutions
are quite - wasted

Drake is making
billions
not on gangsta

we feel the beat
of the traffic
in the city

and your lips

are shiny metal

not soft pastry

Secret

Let's meet on the other side

                        of lust

Just before

                the rain pours in from the west.

We will fold

                our want in linen napkins

and conspire

                with the jasmine.

Untitled

I kneel in the pew
with stained glass eyes

with more questions
than I have answers.

Can healing be found
in layers of lost prayers?

Hope Street

when you're feeling
quite alone

and you've dropped the yarn
from the valley of your apron

hang your heart
with pins on clotheslines

and plant tulips
in the cuffs of your blue jeans

Bubbling

It's not just a cup of tea.

It's a love affair with warmth.

It's a morning metamorphosis.

It's an afternoon flirtation.

It's liquid hands on chipped china.

It's my mother dipping a Lipton tea bag.

It's my grandfather sipping County Cork

- where the sweetness settles in.

Shepherd

when words fail you

be the instrument of peace

listen to the lamb's ear

tend your flock

herd your nouns and verbs

to where the hill breaks

though the captured soon escape

for the stone walls in County Kerry

cannot contain your mystique

Twilight

It's the glass hour.

Light softens.

The flat house marches.

Slowly.

Into the lake.

Black mirror.

Frozen

The woods
are in repose.

A doe blends.
I stand, a mannequin.

White settles
on holy ground.

We stare
unblinking.

Snow falls.
She flees.

Deer tracks.
A halo circles the sun.

Fanfare

the leaves are changing

twin birds on a wire sing

the euphony of seasons past and nigh

wind whips

                day dives

                                the yellow drowns

drip, drip of color

as a scarlet ghost gallops

across the sky

unnoticed by all eyes, except mine

Turning

White season fades
the March sun paints in apricot.

Elders abandon knitted afghans
and the hum of radiators.

Children mourn
the loss of snow forts.

Tulips with their scissor petals,
puncture the swollen sky.

Mother Earth upturns
towards golden light.

Labyrinth

She's not bulletproof,

she's feelings ridden.

She doesn't hiss,

she roars.

Her eyes are forests.

Her heart, a blade.

Her body, a kingdom.

Her cane is a sword and a staff.

She will battle you

and befriend you.

She builds walls and bridges.

She is your wound and your religion.

Pools

I am but water.
The puddle of

last night's shower.
I live for an hour or two.

Until the sunshine
absorbs me.

I am the ocean
for children in Wellington boots.

For earthworms.
And for the descent of errant swallows.

I am the pavement's
liquid memory.

I am a silver mirror.
Reflecting.

Maybe I Was Wrong

You weren't the violence
of a storm.

Or the empty sky,
disfigured.

Maybe you were
a thousand doves.

The Sistine Chapel.
Or the sea

surging
maybe you were beauty

untamed.

Springtime in New England

all the leaves

are bathed in gold

all the lawns

are sea of green

all the birds

are sun drops calling

all the roads

of green lead us home

My Haven

I like to go to bookstores
on rainy days
when droplets pelt
the window panes
and the world unbuttons
its slicker

I like to go to bookstores
when the sun bathes
the dusty spines
and a tiger crouches patient
on the upper-most shelf
of the poetry section

Liberation

Today I will
try to free

my faith, caught
in a cloud of branches,

in the white pine
in my back yard.

The Storm

A warm summer rain begins to fall.
I could run home or tilt my head and swallow
the sky.

Starlit

boardwalk ends
seagulls flee
a couple shares
silly talk beneath the moon

his silken lips
kiss thighs
and hips
rapid fall of sundress

his fingers press
her sunburned skin
the rise her chest
a summer spent
- drowning

Virginia Woolf

she was the daughter of anger
and a child of tolerance

she could not, would not
bite her tongue

her words were the army
her poetry, the battleground

and as I watched her type
I realized her hands were political,
her fingers justice

Bathing

The skylight is open
I stand knee deep in stars,
you are framed by a silver moon.

The tub is clawfoot.
You slide in, I pull your hair back
and run the water.

Violets

Your body is a summer fever
a meadow of soft curves.

I am high on your
pistil and petals.

You are reading Plath
and I am camping in your lap.

You are a
purple symphony.

I keep pulling you nearer
than skin to me.

The sky spills
gentle blue desire.

Polaroid

she tilts her head
within the photograph

she grips your heart
within the frame

nothing in the image
is an accident

little invitations
spilled out

she's the girl who speaks
without a tongue

every kiss a revelation
every touch without a doubt

Depth

meet me in the place where there are no words

just the ocean and the blue of us

Not Fancy

Mary Oliver's hands
wrap around a Mason jar

in Provincetown
white tulips bloom in January.

Poems scud along
her eyes full of sky.

She journals with
a number 2 pencil.

Writing in cursive,
a rehearsal of love.

A fleet of daffodils
and pinwheels sail by.

Love Song

I want to read poetry with only you

in a certain coffee shop

in East Cambridge

when it snows

words pulse a duet

backlit

real slow

these are our lyrics

with notes blue

poetry that tastes like jazz

music's rhythm at the core of me and you

A Meadow of Junes

let's puncture the blue sky today

pluck the swollen fruit

spread a blanket

fold napkins made of Queen Anne's Lace

pick candy colored lupine

have a banquet

eat gooseberry pie

sip claret colored potions

dance under a steeple of pine trees

Sensory

I want to publish a book filled with poems that you can't read

you will have to touch them

you will have to breathe them in

the poems will be so small

they will be written on the hearts of hummingbirds

they will be so elegant that they will bloom

in the mouths of flowers

Untitled

I know the echo
of the little things.

I've seen the ripple
In the pond's rings.

I've heard the euphony
when the robin sings.

I have loved
the wellsprings.

I don't believe
in angel's wings.

But I've heard
the refrain of my heart strings.

And you, you
are everything.

Winning

there's a certain beauty in defeat
a grace in losing right

when the blood of knuckles
scrapes the field of battle
and the emptiness rings true

then the loss is not a tragedy
but a sweet suffering

a truth that echoes hard

Collide

If you crash into me

I may become you

and if I wander near the shore

I may become the sea

Company

when I die I will sit
on the edge of your mind
- patient

think of this –
the faith of our sky
lifts the dawn

you may doubt your gods;
question your religion

winds may batter
storms may slam

but my hands are there
to catch you
– from beyond

Awakening

I abandon
cherished sunshine

for candlelit vespers.

Praying hands,
my holy

treasure.
My faith

           it bends.

This gap
is filled.

Time is slowly
measured.

The voice

of Providence,

it wakes

it speaks.

A sacred pause,

I listen.

Desperation

she was walking towards the sea
so I took the stones from her pockets

Aubade

sunlight grazes her body

morning blankets fall

her eyes are closed

a spin of color

a spill of violets

liquid breakfast

a stillness we devour

we breathe slower

escape beneath the surface

blue lovers

Folly

let's create a third person

a space between us

a meadow
where wildflowers grow

let's inhabit:

>the skin and bones of love
>the thorn and rose of love
>the "I suppose" of love

Innocence

He is eight
months old

and I dance
on the treetops

for him.
The glow rises in

his face
like a halo.

His legs kick up
like Maradona.

He parachutes
into my arms.

The shape of
joy landing.

Nurture

to have a child is to plant your heart

in a garden and watch those hopeful shoots grow

What is truth?

but the thread that clings
to the cloak of God

- and I hang on

Sinking

The shadow of your hair
swallows waning sunlight.

I can almost taste you,
your late summer skin.

Your breath is pressing
against my chest

You pull me under,
eyes of moon.

I move closer,
you remind me

to discover
the bend of your neck

is shifting
the hands of time.

The night is melting

surge of tides.

Untitled

I write you poetry / we make babies often /
on Sundays / I taste hyacinth /
your collarbone / our puppy is born from a
shy crate / you tell me stories over coffee /
we plan our genealogy / we Hulu, Prime, Netflix /
you couch me / sometimes I want chocolate
on my chocolate /I want you / always

Untitled

maybe hope is a world

where our children grow into flowers

deeply rooted

Divination

she picks wild flowers
for her pleasure

a crown adorns her
queen of hearts

she takes what she wants
from The Giving Tree

she doesn't need a man
nor Tarot Cards to have a future

she channels her own energies:
The Magician, The Empress, and The Chariot.

Solstice

in late June

you can taste

the tip of the sky

the faeries

weave ribbons

of blue

and the window boxes

invite dragonflies

to the show

even the primrose

slips out

of her vase

and the cardinals

paint the scene

in scarlet

Untethered

and I kiss her
in the molten hours

when the sun
slips into the sea

we feel the breath
of tides

and love
is a vibration

we skip stones
across the universe

two bodies surge
on endless waters

I Love You

how the sun melts into the horizon

how the moon holds midnight

how the sea grips the shore

soul first

Molecular

If you are mostly made up of water
then I am deeply in love with the sea

Acknowledgements

I would like to thank Helen Cox, my first editor. Working with her has been a privilege.

I would also like to thank all of my supporters/friends on social media.

Joe Barca

Biography

Joe Barca is a husband, a father, and the owner of a wheaten terrier. He has published three short poetry collections – *A Picnic Moon*, *Henry & Grace: A Love Story & Other Poetry*, and *My Therapist is a Couch*. He is a fast talker and a slow runner. He lives in New England.

You can follow Joe on Twitter @shepherdmoon53 and on Instagram at poetblacksmith.

Joe Barca

www.ingramcontent.com/pod-product-compliance
Lightning Source LLC
Chambersburg PA
CBHW021957290426
44108CB00012B/1113